Grateful

A Song of Giving Thanks

To all those who choose love instead of fear
—J.B.

To my husband Reino, and to Julia, Frans, and Veeti,
who keep me inspired
—A.L.H.

ISBN 0-439-83665-4

"Grateful" words and music by John Bucchino.
Copyright © 1996 by John Bucchino.
Art Food Music owner of publication and allied rights throughout
the world (administered by Williamson Music). International Copyright secured.
Illustrations copyright © 2003 by Anna-Liisa Hakkarainen. All rights reserved.
Published by Scholastic Inc., 557 Broadway, New York, NY 10012,
by arrangement with HarperCollins Publishers. SCHOLASTIC and associated logos
are trademarks and/or registered trademarks of Scholastic Inc.

12 11 10 9 8 7 6 5 4 3 2 1   5 6 7 8 9 10/0

Printed in the U.S.A.   66

First Scholastic printing, November 2005

Typography by Jeanne L. Hogle

Grateful

A Song of Giving Thanks

By John Bucchino • Illustrated by Anna-Liisa Hakkarainen

The Julie Andrews Collection

SCHOLASTIC INC.

New York Toronto London Auckland Sydney
Mexico City New Delhi Hong Kong Buenos Aires

I've got a roof over my head.

I've got a warm place to sleep.

Some nights I lie awake counting gifts

Instead of counting sheep.

I've got a heart that can hold love.

I've got a mind that can think.

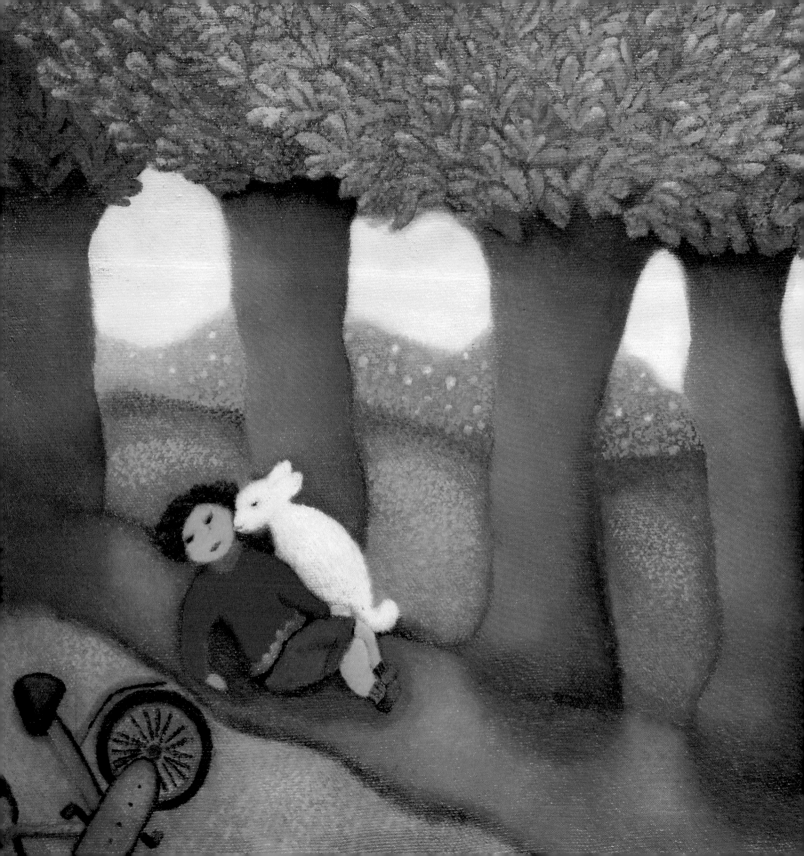

There may be times when I lose the light

And let my spirits sink . . .

But I can't stay depressed

When I remember how I'm blessed!

Grateful, grateful

Truly grateful I am.

Grateful, grateful

Truly blessed

And duly grateful.

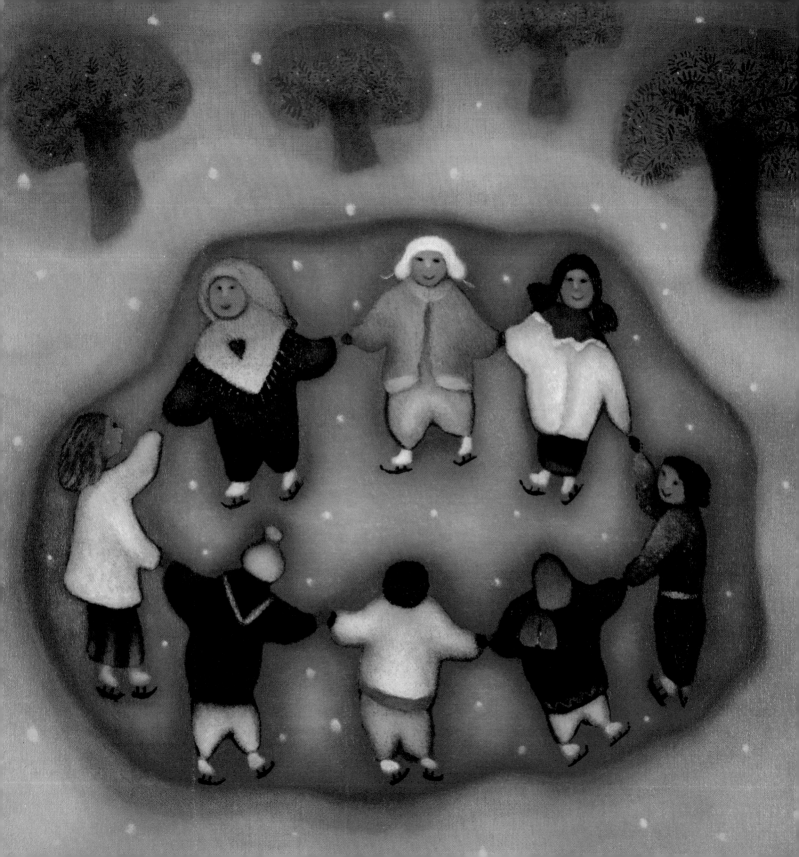

In a city of strangers,

I've got a family of friends.

No matter what rocks and brambles

    fill the way,

I know that they will stay until the end.

I feel a hand holding my hand.

It's not a hand you can see.

But on the road to the promised land

This hand will shepherd me . . .

Through delight and despair,

Holding tight and always there.

Grateful, grateful

Truly grateful I am.

Grateful, grateful

Truly blessed

And duly grateful.

It's not that I don't want a lot,

Or hope for more or dream of more.

But giving thanks for what I've got

Makes me so much happier than keeping score.

In a world that can bring pain,

I will still take each chance . . .

For I believe that whatever the terrain

Our feet can learn to dance.

Whatever stone life may sling,

We can moan . . .

Or we can sing!

Grateful, grateful

Truly grateful I am.

Grateful, grateful

Truly blessed

And duly grateful.

Truly blessed

And duly grateful.

Grateful

Words and Music by
JOHN BUCCHINO

Steady 4, Reverently (♩ = 72)

p I've got a roof o-ver my head, ___

mp sempre legato

With pedal

I've got a warm place ___ to sleep. Some nights I lie a-wake ___ count-ing gifts ___ in-stead

___ of count-ing sheep. ___ I've got a heart that ___ can hold ___ love, ___

I've got a mind that can think. There may be times when I ___ lose ___ the light ___ and let ___

___ my spir-its sink. ___ But I can't stay ___ de-pressed ___ when I re-mem-ber ___ how I'm

NOTE: This is a simplified version of the sheet music of the song "Grateful." The complete version may be found in the songbook *GRATEFUL: The Songs of John Bucchino*, available at www.johnbucchino.com